This Book Belongs To

CON YOU COLOR THESE ANIMALS?

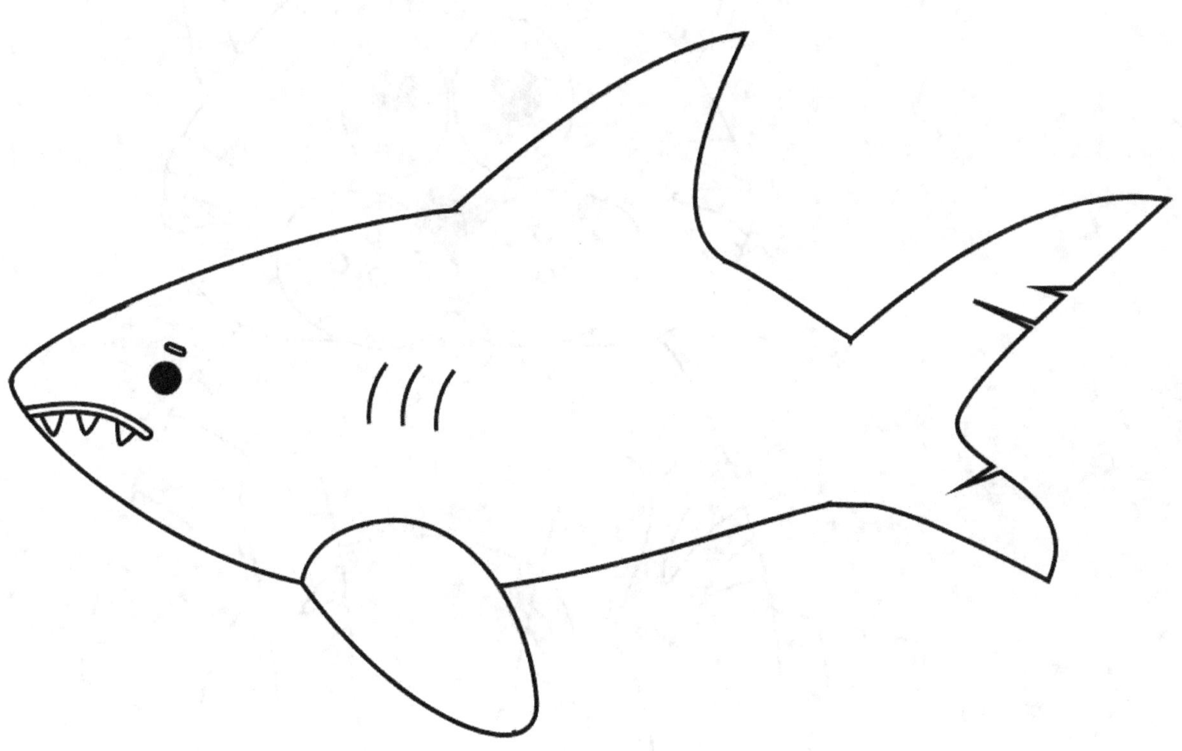

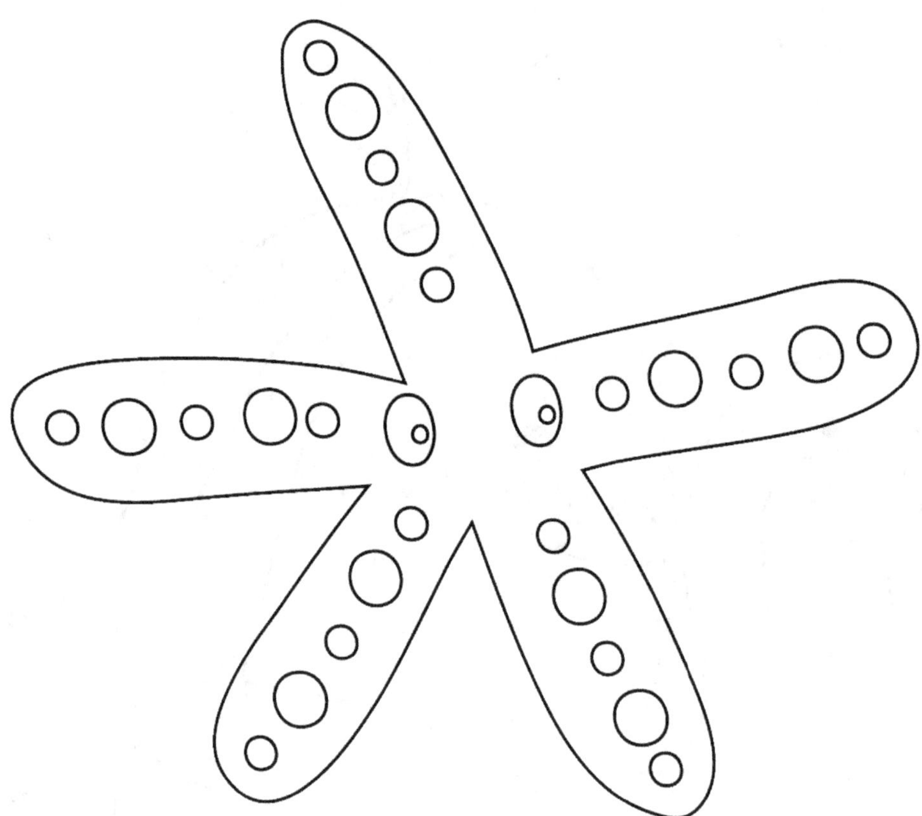

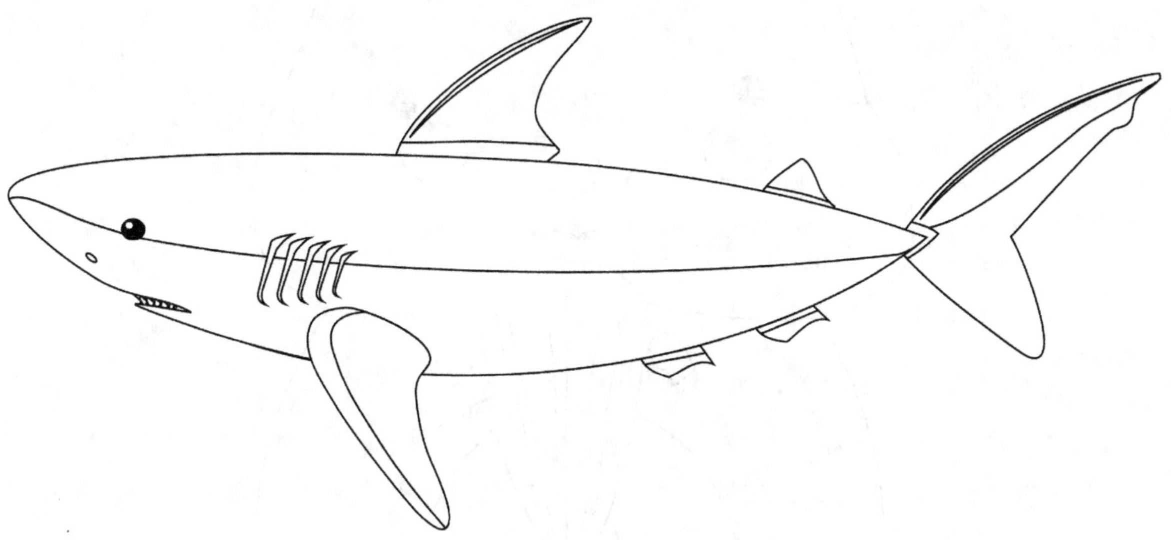

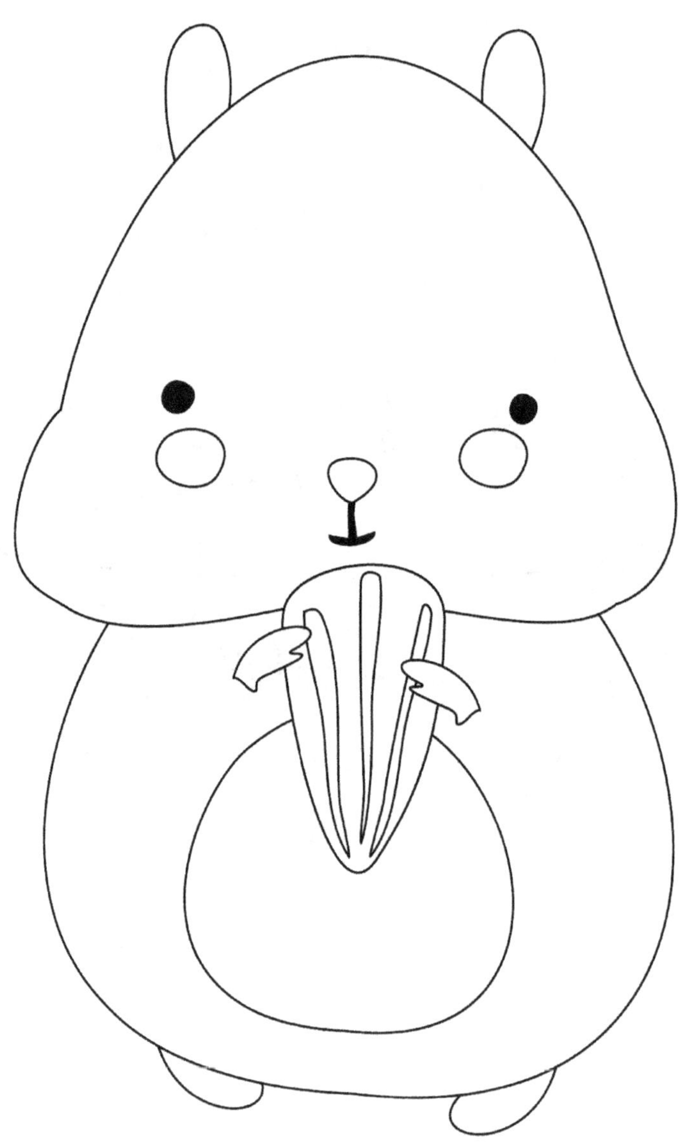

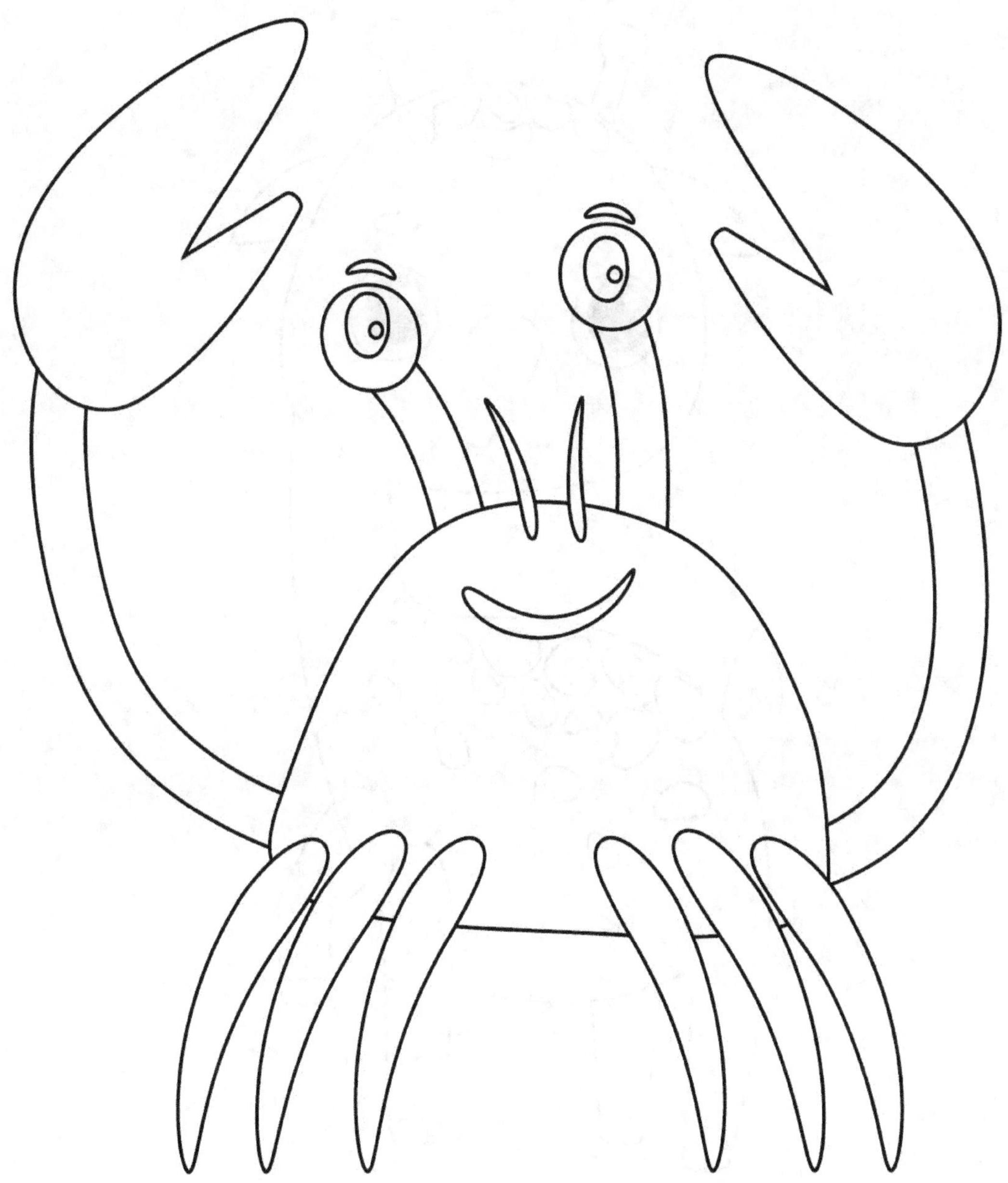

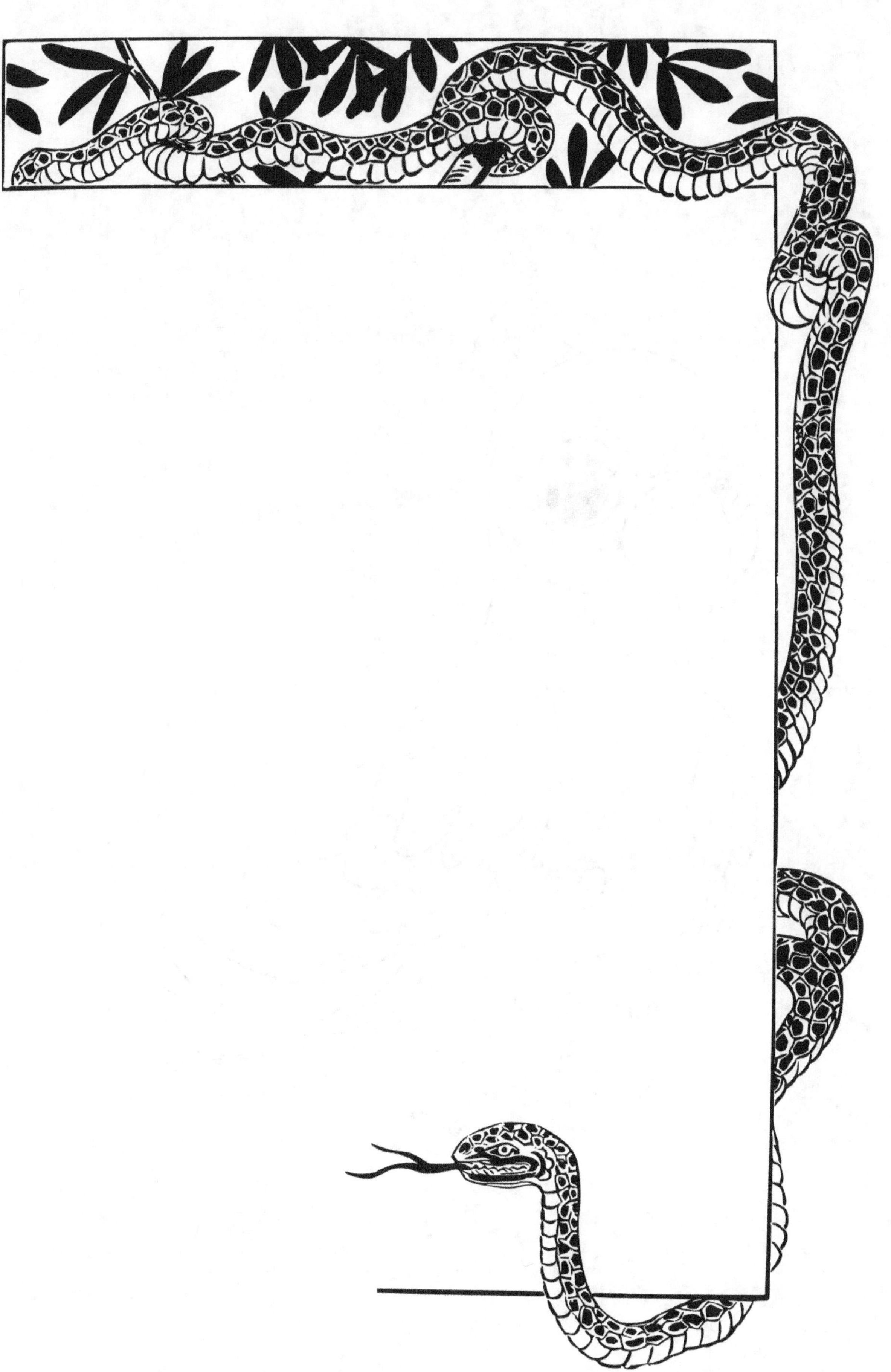

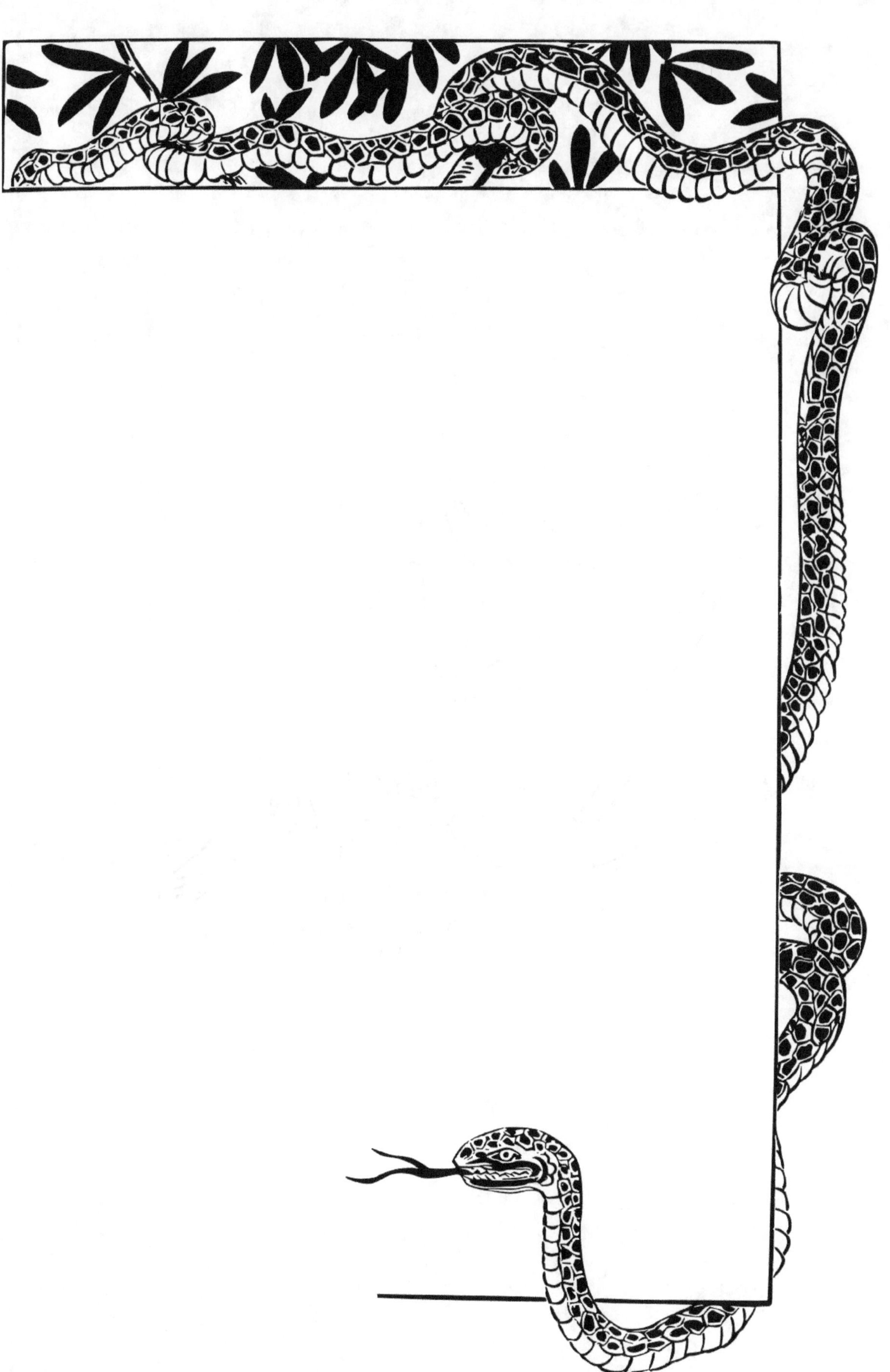

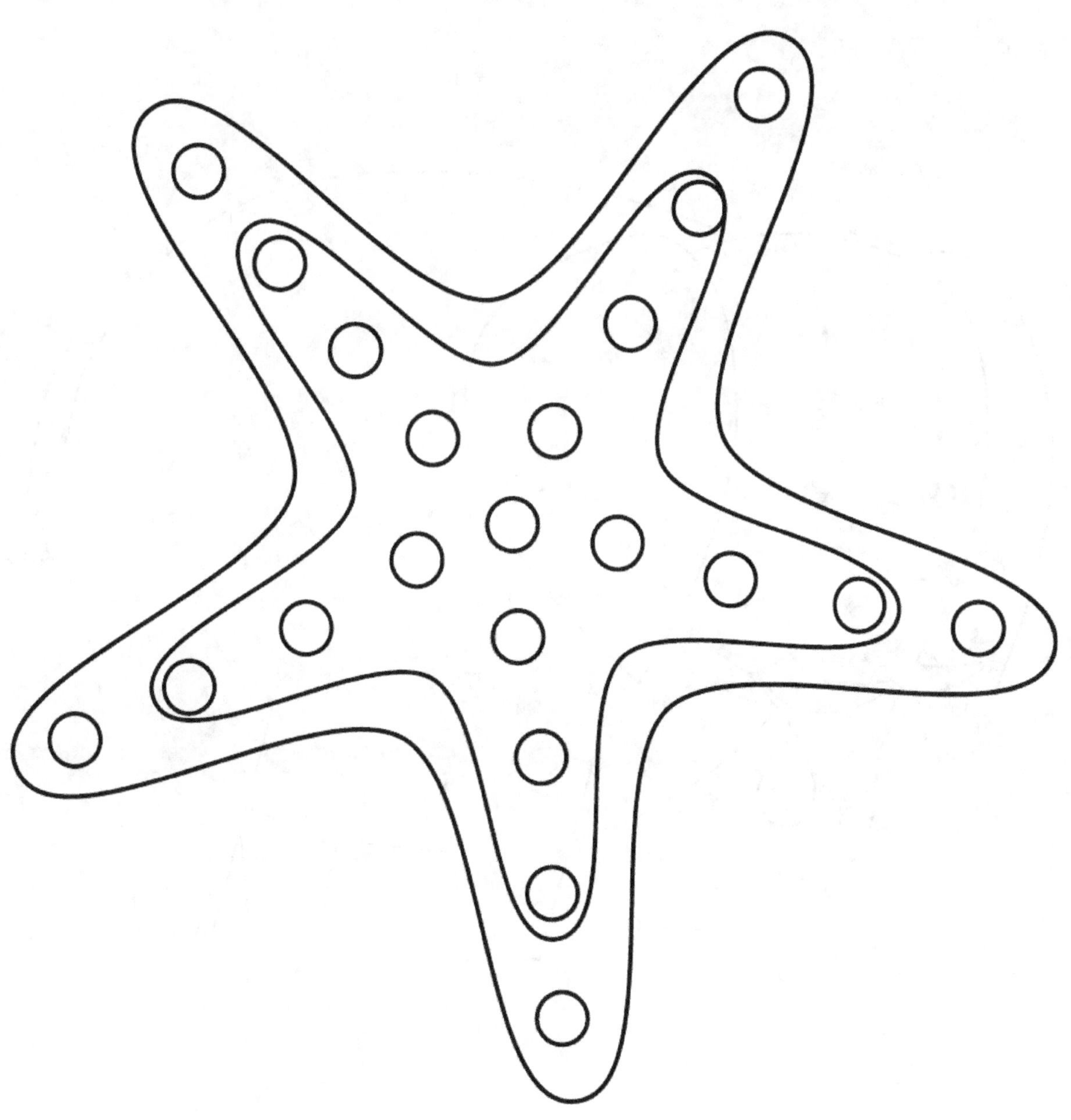

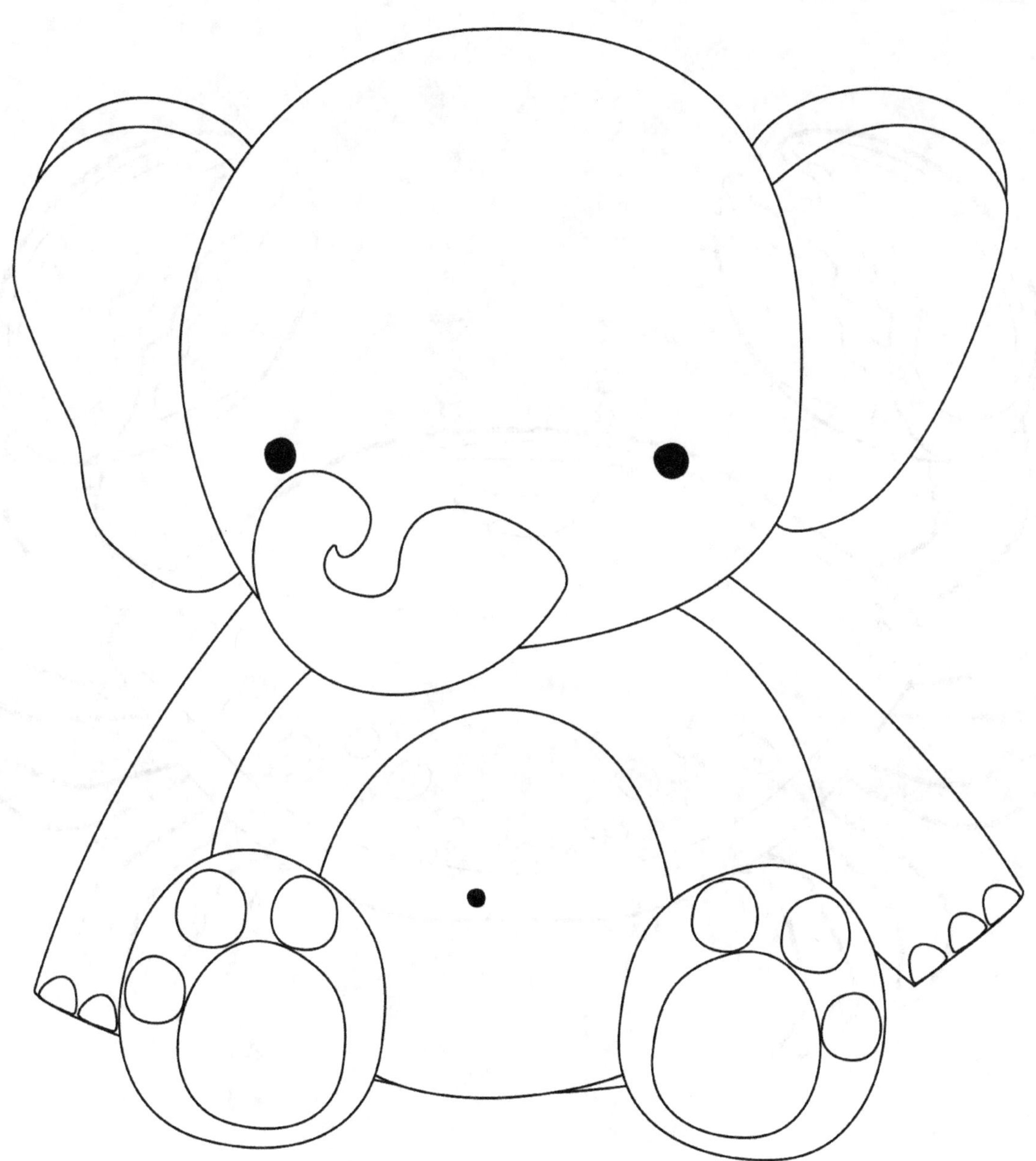

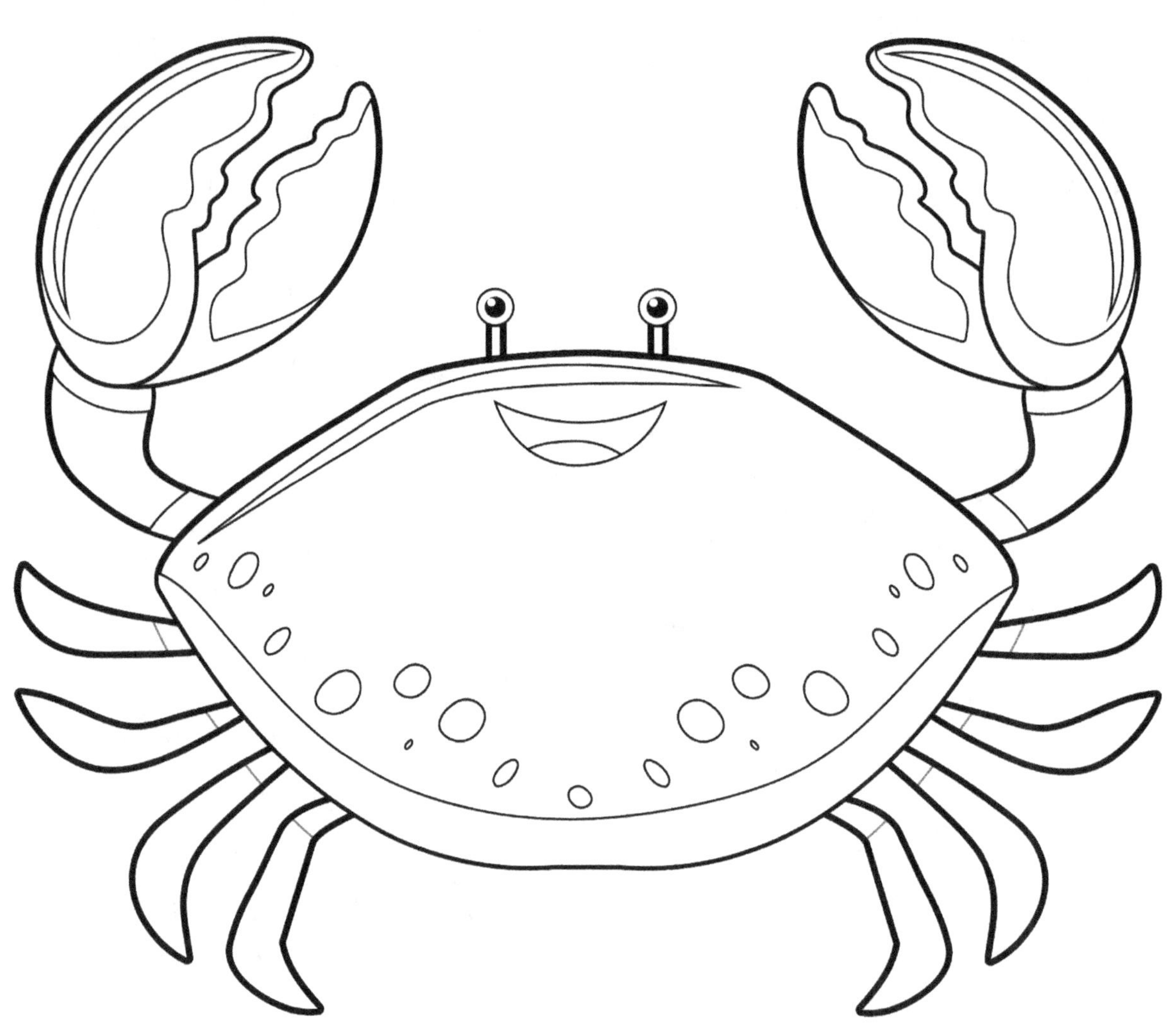

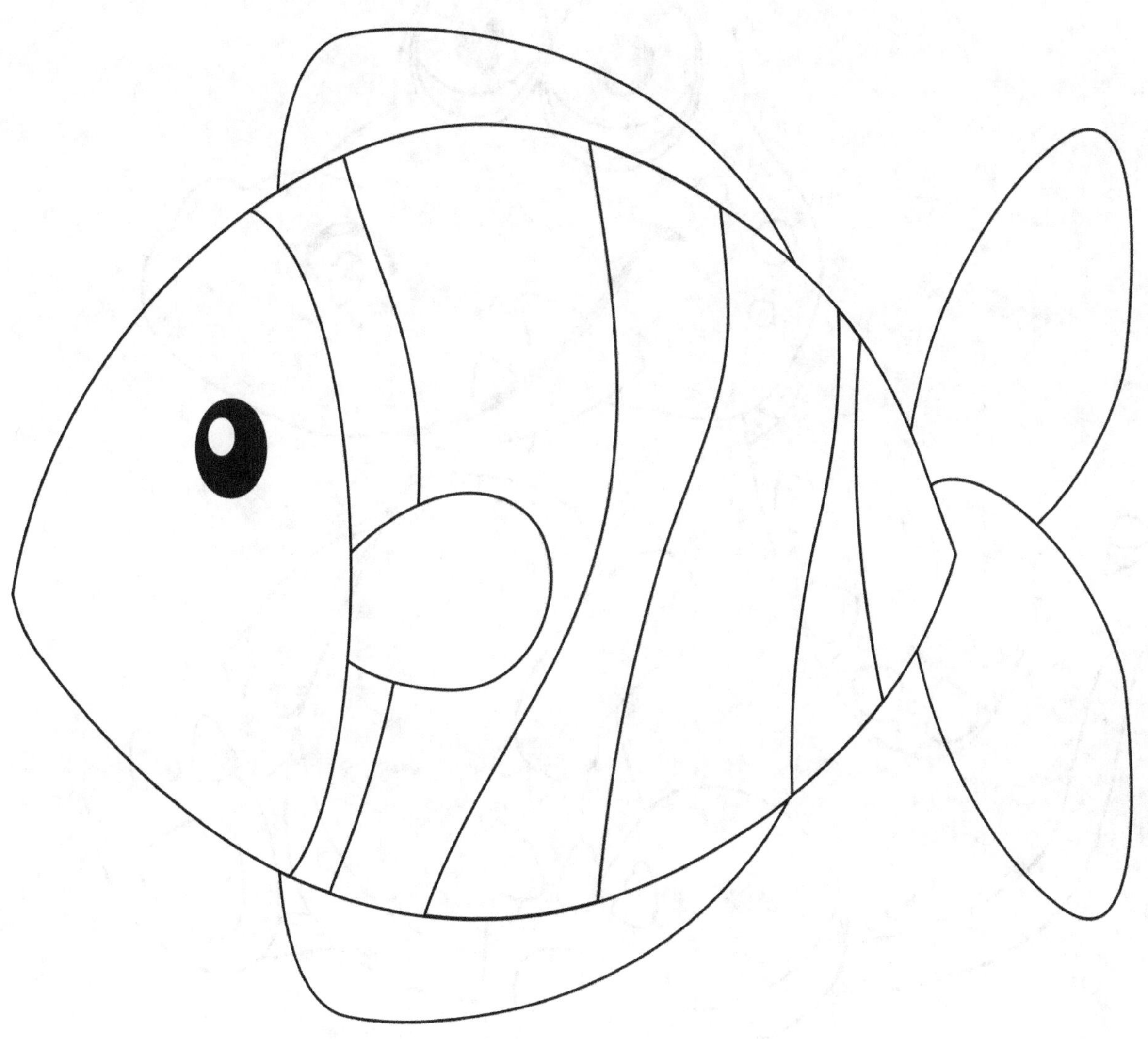

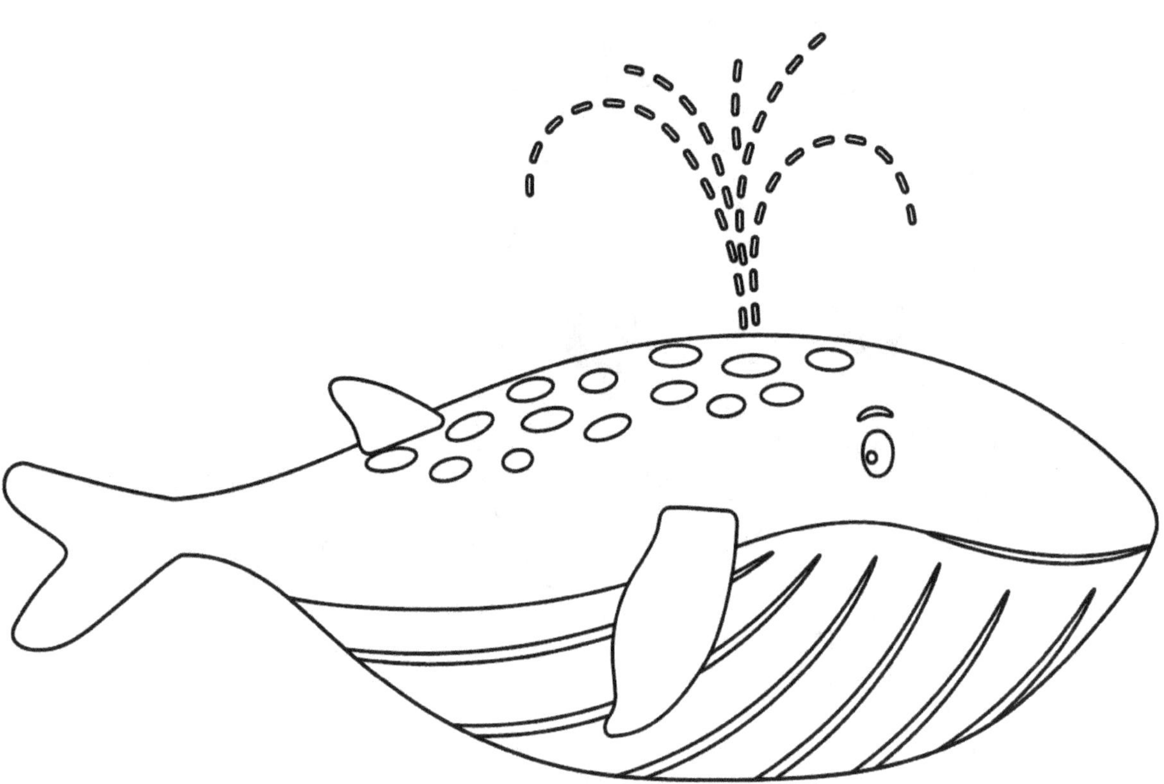

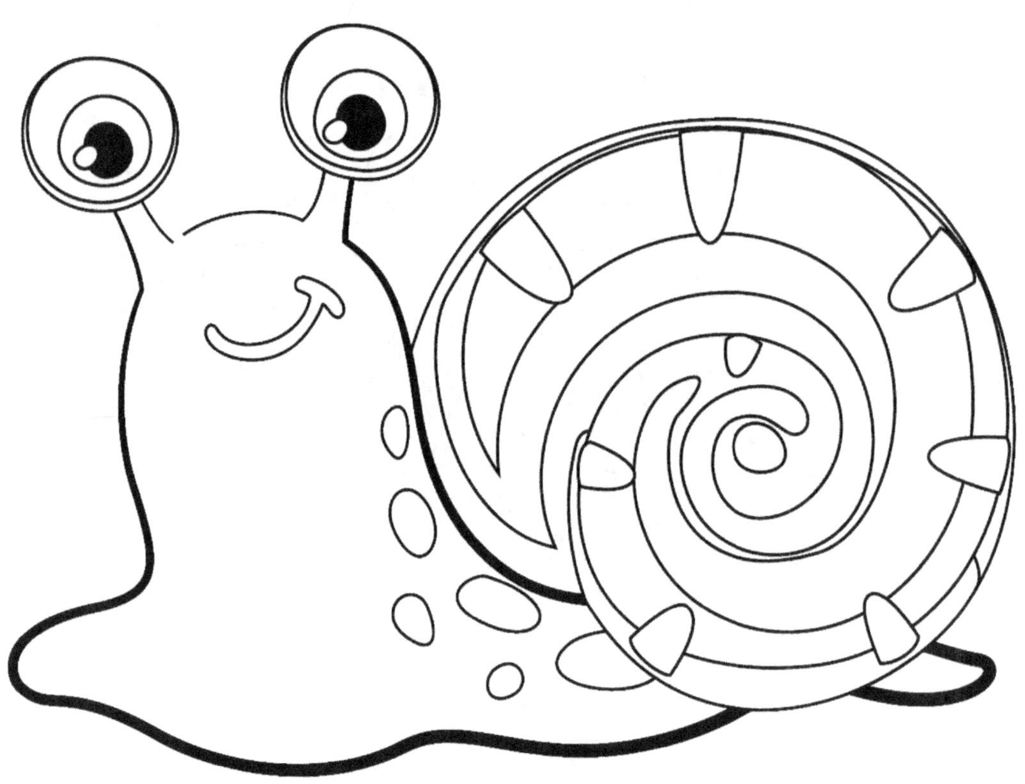

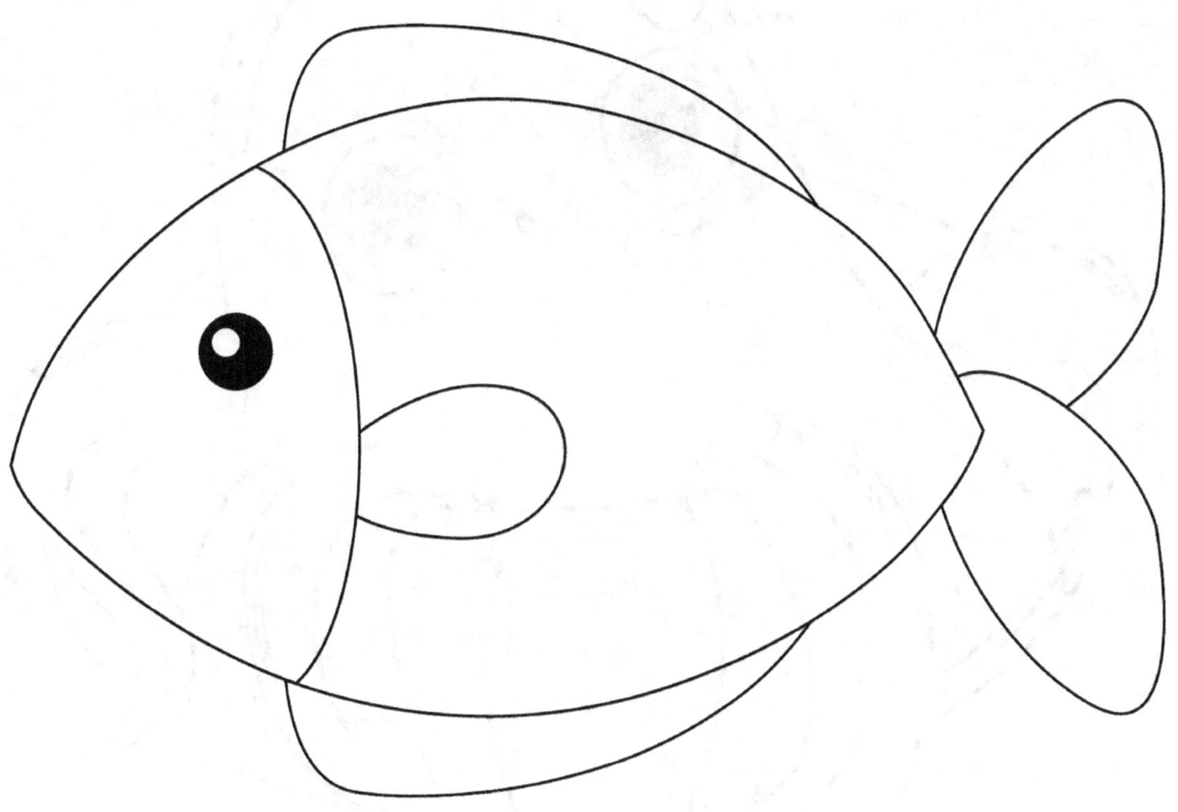

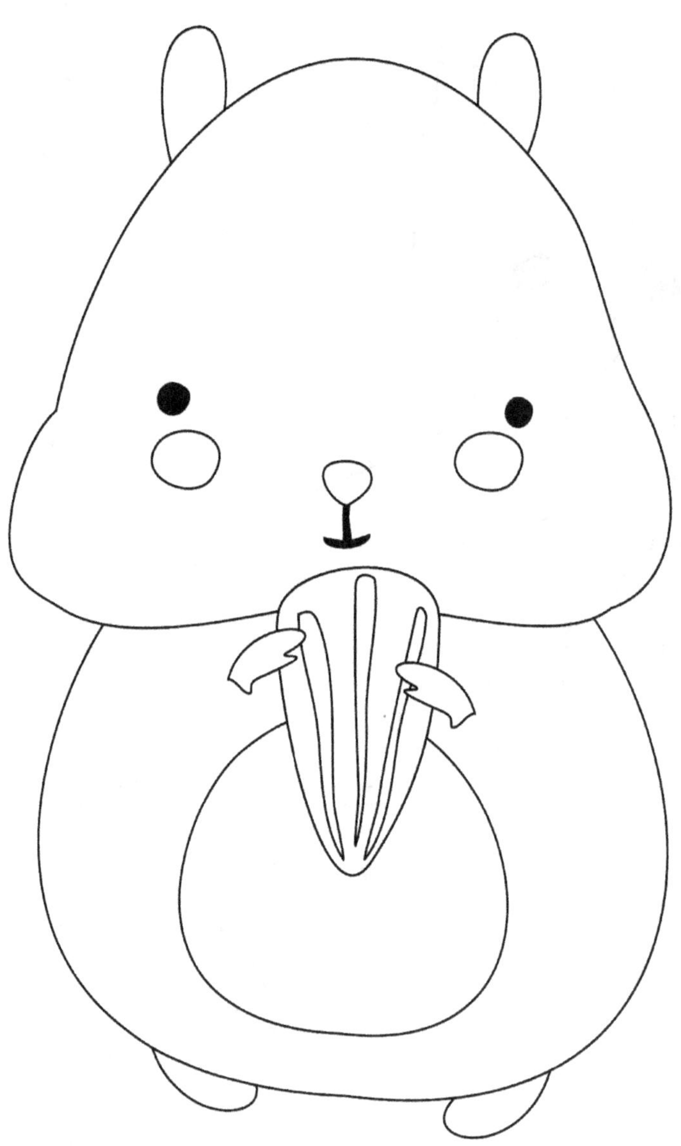